OF THE HEART AND SOUL
– A MELLIFLUOUS WHISPER

A garland of verses
by
PIYALI MITRA

First Published in March 2021

ISBN: 978-93-5427-608-8

BLUEROSE PUBLISHERS

www.bluerosepublishers.com

info@bluerosepublishers.com

+91 8882 898 898

Cover Design:

Joshua Freitas

Typographic Design:

Namrata Saini

Distributed by: BlueRose, Amazon, Flipkart, Shopclues

Preface

Emotions it is said are what makes us human and we have been experiencing them since our inception to this world of living. Emotion in various form remarkably has been unveiled in Literature but of all love and pain stood out among all the emotions. Pain is modulated by various conditions, the most notable of which is emotions. Since love is an emotion, it can also modulate pain. The answer to the reflection whether love mitigate or aggrandize pain is subject to determination and examination.

This anthology abounds in the feeling of love-- Love has always been the source of inspiration for the countless poems and thoughtful scribbling made by lovers and admirers, but few poems are written analyzing the concept and how to feel to be in love. This book speaks of how love can be the source of inspiration at the same time the source of abjection. Rejection and dejection can push one to corner while love can uplift and transcend mind from one realm to another. This garland of verses as the author would love to call is also a memory book remembering the various emotions her mother has been subjected to. The author's mother like other mommas have always inspired and influenced thoughts of her child. She has been a silent struggler and has never left her guard of endurance, patience and grace down. As a tribute to her contribution in shaping the author's life and thought she has penned a poetry as an ode to her Mamma.

In fact, the range of styles and movements employed throughout the collection of verses may appear to underscore how the genre constantly evolves and transforms as the author made a conscious effort to capture the essence of human experience.

Some lines and verses of this book speak the loudest and most directly and others have reflection of vibrant imagery and artful characters. Some lines have divine intonation while others draw heavily from mundane. The author personally feels tolerance to a certain limit is permitted beyond that we need to hit hard where need be and words and lines are powerful weapon to translate the feeling. The author being the artist herself draws inspiration from Nature. The book has tried to capture the colors, aroma and essences of water, land, mountains, seasons and even leaves. Every object of Nature has their own language. The book has endeavoured to communicate that subtle language through verses.

Wordsworth has once noted that the power requisite for penning poetry is the ability to observation and fidelity to description. The author is deeply inspired by this belief of Wordsworth. However, it depends upon the readers to judge whether she has been able to justify in the portrayal and making of attractive poetic description.

The author hopes that each of the poems of this anthology would provide refreshing thoughts for her readers and they would be wanting for more in future.

Desiring compassion, blessings and warmth of thoughts for the endeavor.

Piyali Mitra

Acknowledgement

No words would be enough to express my gratitude to those people who helped me in making my dream to publish my poetry book come true. I would expressly like to thank my parents Sati and Sunil Kumar Mitra for always standing by me and making me believe that I can write and dream and that dreams can always become real. Thank you my dearest young sister Chaitali Mitra (Rinky) for encouraging me always and keep loving me as if we are one soul. Thanks are due to Kaustuv Ray Dada, a theatrician and author of Bengali plays who constantly has positive and constructive message for my work. Thanks are due to Shruti Goswami, a prolific writer and poet herself for her review of the poem "*Garden—a solace of the soul*". I would remain thankful to my father-in-law Dr Suchit Sur for his belief in me.

I would also like to thank Naval Commander Ritwik Chatterjee, dear Bulan da for showing immense respect in my abilities and to be my inspiration in life and dream. Thanks to Professor Priyambada Sarkar, of the University of Calcutta for giving me the space to pursue my dream even in the tight research schedule. Thanks also to my husband for his constant support and to the great Almighty God.

Last but not the least, I would express my sincerest gratitude to the Blue Rose Publication Team with special mention of Publication Consultant, Isha and Publication Manager, Bhanupriya. This anthology would have never seen the light had it not being for their kind and efficient assistance.

Dedicated

To

Ma, Baba and

My dear sister Rinky

Contents

Contents

Garden—Solace of the Soul.

I look out to my garden
It transfixes and transports me
Into a world of beauty and color,
A sanctuary of peace and ecstasy.
Where lovely things mix and match.

As fresh morning unfolds
The flowers nod their sleepy heads.
The dew drops fall from leaves of plants,
Reflecting the glorious sunshine.

Parallel helixes, winding all around,
Soft shrouds caress the skin,
Spiraling pine dancing and whirling,
Rolling as a feather on the ground.

The green and yellow papaya hang low.
Some small, some tall,
Straight trunk with no branch to grow,
Dangling large-palm like leaves
Swinging gently in the breeze.

The bottle palm head held high and tall,
Defying nature's rage and furious call.
The scented lime gives a fresh presumption,
The rounded long gourd peeping from the green junctions.

The cilantro whisper pass from grass to grass,
The frugal curry leaves dazzling in the auburn sun.
Seeds of carrot and okra
Fostered and nurtured below the earth.

Creepers sauntering on the flower bed about to be raked,
Slumbering peonies feigning to stay awake.

Impatiens in jaded pink and red burst forth,
Inca, Dianthus, Narcissus, Ferns
With outspread fronds, waiting to take an oath.
The Hibiscus, Calendula non-sentient is ever smiling,
With petals of vibrant hues and nectar filling.

I walk around savouring each aromatic smell,
Scattering sweet alyssum that smells like honey and love
Throughout the soft air.
This garden where love blooms like a flower,
Not overgrown with bitter weeds and rue,
A treasure-trove where friends grow,
Where distraught minds and souls of the world find ease.

This garden where life goes on,
Filling empty spaces when the old plant gone.
A soothing balm for troubled heart.

This is where I tread into—
A retreat of peace crossing
Dignified borders and stretches of wood away
I find tangles of happy disorder.

Existence Alarm.

A new day heralds us all
As if after a stormy night has come a tranquil day of preparedness.

Is everything that is evil just black?
Is white the symbol of righteousness and innocence?

Well if life is symbolized by pristine white
And death, if you are marked as awful black
Then why that white creature, nay that white virus?
Pulled you down and knelt on your neck
Until you pleaded, "I can't breathe"

If everything that is black is inauspicious,
Then why the dark-skinned Krishna is the apple of every eye?
Why is Kali, the dark Goddess revered and adulated?

Black, you have been thrashed and assaulted day after day,
But you, who has accentuated those pair of eyes.
You, the shadow that accompany every being on Earth,
You, the constant companion in good and bad times together.

You hide no truth, you are not ugly
You dare to wear the armour on your sleeves.

Wake up now the voice is raised
You will no longer be addressed with impudence,
Let's move together and forget the differences.

The war against discrimination is waged
The bugle resonates but hark!
This cry of melee hope not be fugacious
For we can't afford to lose the 'Dark' Wantons, George Floyds, and Mike Browns

Nay, it's time to turn around
For the alarm of existence is reverberating

Every life matters.

The Unseen...

The day walked with her,
Gliding by the walkway and nook covered in green.
Sitting as the sun dropped by the other side,
She looked beyond the culvert.

When the day passed the baton to the night
The hum of the cicada in cadence,
The sway of first bloom in a row.
The shape of the lamp's illumination in the room.
Night waits, it glides in tiptoeing,
Forsaking every gloom.

For hark,
She sleeps in comfort and peace.
Her eyes grow heavy and her heart warm.
She falls into an enchanting slumber.
Those drooping eyes, those parting lips,
Entwining and embracing the observer in close grips.

The lamp watches, relinquishes dark forlorn,
As slumber night gives way to a waking morn,
As light cascading from heaven to earth below.
Unseen, unheard dust of letters blow up,
Twirling in delight from hidden hedges,

Speaks of stories of mellifluous dulcet
Cooing behind the ears.

The day the words were heard and the song of love rekindled
He picked them up and punctuated them into the soul.
Those words that stuck deep within, would never let you go....

A Fallen Leaf

She fluttered, she swayed in the gust.
With kid-like steps she plied.
Unsure, uncertain her podgy hands grip the hem.
Those peeping, dreamy azure eyes whooshing love.
As honeysuckle brimming sweetness full.

But alas!
She falls in the dreary wintry wind,
None to hold her trembling body,
Her wings clipped.
Brown, crimson, yellow she wears and changes into
And helter-skelter she pranced by.

But now,
With moistened eyes she looks up.
Where lies her roots, her haven gone
With a last reminiscence of her swing,
She falls, her dreams lost,
In the zephyr of autumnal mellifluous lullaby.
She sighs with a heavy heart.

Love - An Inspiration.

They say
Love is a mellifluous song
That needs two souls
That beat in unison.
They are voices that coos in gesture and silence,
Love is the best of all emotion
Unpolluted and sparkling,
Like the light of a thousand diamonds,
Love creates rainbows and ripples of affections.

But then
Love is not a magnet
There are some undrafted songs,
Those lines are lost forever.
Love sometime feels like shards and splinters,
That when pierced with, bleeds profusely.
Music, country roads and future dreams
Loose their way in the dark unconscious oblivion.

However,
Love is all about hope and faith.
It demands patience and nurture,
It is no mere bewitching spell
That once found and lost forever.

Love is a song that heals and puts the gaping wounds to sleep.
Cherish every moment of togetherness
Through the laughter and tears of joy,
And breathe the sweet summer air.
Love embalms and sets the heart free
And gives the will to live.

To a Loving Heart.

A bell is not a bell
Until someone rings it.
A song is not a song
Until someone sings it.
Beauty is not a joy
Until someone perceives it,
Morning cannot be a beginning
Until it shows the day.
Love wasn't put
In the heart to stay
For love isn't love
Until you give it away.

A Call to Her Soul.

Meera's call,
Lord, I send letters to my *Beloved,*
My dearest *Krishna.*
But he purposely preserves silence
Sends no reply.
The silence kills me, hurts my soul,
No one understands my plight.
Only a wounded soul
Understands the agonies of the wounded.

When the fire rages in the heart,
It devours every senses.

I have forsaken everything to be one with my Lord.
He is my husband—mine, my own.
I worship the lotus-feet of the Indestructible One!
The world is lost in those two eyes,
That views the world and me.

Lord, it's the Love
That binds me to You
Like the bird
That gazes all night.
At the passing moon.
I have lost myself in You.

Meera calls,
I am sold into your hands,
Kiss those pure lotus-feet with head bowing down
I seek you and only you
For nothing is mine except you.
I have been Thy slave in former births,
Thou art the be-all of my existence.
Lord, how can you remain so far away!

Sweet Dreams.

Tonight as you open your window and gaze the sky
Full of twinkly stars, a veil of a blushing bride.
The riding moon alights softly on earth, peeping into my room.
I lay in my bed holding you tight in mind,
The thoughts running behind my head with every breath that I take.
You've crossed my mind many nights,
I search for you, but none a place you could be found.
The injured soul finds solace in dark loneliness.
I close my eyes, I hear your voice inside my heart,
You whisper to me so elegantly.
As you kiss my forehead.
My heavy head hits the pillow,
Falling asleep,
To the rhythm of your heart beat.
"Sweet dreams — O my sweet one"
While angels keeps our dreams sweet.
I rest now, the breeze upon my face,
I drift far away in the land of warmth and pure bliss.

Ode to a Little Squirrel.

O little one, you have stolen my heart.
You worked your furry way inside.
You seem innocent and frail,
But you do have many antics to tell.
Such fuzzy mitts you fuzzily flail
While prizing creatures, (and your tail)
I can't help but wonder what your next scheme is.
While making mischief in your dreams,
You not only pawed and plundered my room,
But you plundered this lonely soul.

The lonely soul that wanders,
Alone in the white land.
No other as his companion.
The lonely soul wanders.....
Light follows darkness as darkness does light:
the stunned sun halts mid-dance;
Shiva Nataraj
motionless, balancing lightly the luminous and tenebrous,
exhorting us to brave the redeeming depth of the shadow.

Books - A Companion of My Heart.

Book is no less a frigate
Which sails in the sea to a land of enlightenment.

Open a book
And we get transported to a land of magic.
A land of giants and fairies,
Both of the make-believe and true alike.

Books brings us joy and tears
Teaches us to be strong and face the storm without fear.
They are friends who take us far and near
From torrid lands and jungle ways
To lands of sandstorms, snow and hail.

Books are the chests of gold,
Where wealth lies in stories and fact told,
Books never disturb the equilibrium,
But facilitate the rule of the soul.

They stand in a row, hand in hand,
Tall, short in shelves, high and low.
Books etch out road with bumps and bends,
With soothing shelter and words of love grow.

Words, either pierce or are the spirit of life,
Splashing with colours of sweetness,
Dancing all the way to the mind of a naïve.
Swirling and twirling they come alive,
From pages to enlightened and accomplished minds.
Books comforts a hurt soul and brings a smile,
They are better than useless gobbledegook and fripperies.

A Lonely Camaraderie.

A solitary walk down the lane.
Leaves her unsure and uncertain.
She looks around but found no one,
Hollowness sucks her deep.

She looks within and found you smiling,
Beckoning her to embrace and hold her tightly,
Lest you be gone again at a blink.

All alone sitting on the edge of her bed
With hands shielding her face,
With tears tinkling down,
Yearning deep within to get.

Like an empty vessel, like a roaring ocean
Her mouth opens to speak.
But sluice gates of emotion let loose the words.
That gushed and tumbled forth
To fill the surrounding void.

With herself she continues her korero,
Unabated and tirelessly she pushed on
With her daily chores, the pain oozes forth.
Emptiness gnaws deep within, refusing to be gone.

Her swollen eyes gazes and beholds the sky above
She sees a streak of light of hope,
Memories as sweet as nectar,
Enlivens and embalms her in despair.
She lives in hope, she lives for love.

Welcome October.

September have now paved the way for October.
Bien venue ma belle!

The month of carnivals,
It ushers in festivities and joy.
It is the treasurer of the year,
Where all the months leave their bounties to be stored
Before the mountains get dusted with snow,
Before the fallen leaves change to brown and yellow,
Before the drooping flowers hung their head low.
We see Nature all aglow.

Nature wears a garment so colourful,
The soft calm playful October sunshine
Kisses the dewy grass beneath.
The pristine white clouds float by,
The rain washed earth fresh out of his bath.
Looks vibrant and dolled up.
It is the prime time before Nature sheds her glory.
Labour accomplished, crops awaiting to be harvested
The drooping cherry bows down to kiss.
Salve October with a myriad bliss.

Since the day I met you.

I realise you were the one
Staring into your face.
A perfect dream soars through my mind,
I felt as if God answered my prayers.
You came as a gift from above.

My heart loses its power,
This love consumes my every breath.
Overpowering my soul,
I pray to be bonded to you in emotional bliss.
United with the soul and seeking refuge in love
Many a times in dreams and fantasies.
My deepest conviction holds
That heaven rests in your loving arms.

But alas! now I realise you are a distant soul,
Far too away to be touched.
You are extraordinary dear,
A brilliant star illuminating the sky above.
You have always made me feel that I was never before,
Your care and love touches the lives around you.
I procrastinate with shaking knees.

Your words enliven me
Your thoughts brings a thousand smiles on my face.
If only you had ever known,
I have had loved you all these years and still so,
With not just my soul,
But with all my being.

With every inch of flesh
And bone in my body.
And every ounce of love instilled in me,
I relinquish my heart forever to you.

It's only in dreams I am bonded in love with you,
But my love will never bind you.
You are a free bird, fly high above and merge with your true soul-mate.
I truly seek your well-being, happiness and good health.
Your great beautiful mind, however would continue
To touch upon a meagre soul like mine.
You would always smother me in your brilliant wings of unfettered love
And flap them in sorceress land,
Though they are dreams yet the dreams I would cherish lifelong.

Twilight Whispers.

If morning is restless youth, twilight
A blushing demure bride.

If morning shows the day, twilight
Promises a balmy twinkling night.

If the early sunshine entering the dappled East
Sets the earth to motion and work,
The rosy crimson twilight puts the demure West
To shiver in delight and kisses her sleepy eyes,
"Goodbye"

Twilight, the threshold of a day to another one
As night creeps across the darkening vale,
The drooping flowers and buds waiting to be reborn
The trees across the field fades into shadowy skies as pale.

The distant house bellowing the chimney smoke,
Where family gathers to taste the evening tea and joke,
The smell of freshly baked buns,
Reminiscence of love, satisfaction we so much yearn.
The mundane melts away in the symphony of colours up in the sky,
The cricket prepares for night gala, and fireflies blow

Their torches to relieve the darkness and deep sigh,
As chirping birds whispers the song of love.

Secrets unfurl like vapour clouds,
Calm crepuscular curtain meets the blue-moon,
Squidgy velvet shine daubs the earth in a romantic shroud,
Dances and twirls for the night is to tiptoe down soon.

Love - Lies - Bleeding.

The red beauty, the mangled hair of Shiva;
A weird looking flower.

It looks so alien, they are
Heirloom flowers.

Brilliant red seed heads dangle
Like shimmering ruby necklaces.

The immortal 'amarantha' promises undying love,
By Jove, the touch of this prince's feather is so soft,

The love-lies-bleeding blooms in richer shades,
Crimson tassels cascade to the ground
Like a braid of a lovely maid.

The jewel of the garden, stoops down
Day after day, as months pass by and frown.

Uncomplaining it droops kissing the earth below
In utter languishment he hangs his head so low.

The dew kisses its soft brows, in an embracing haunt,
The undying Gladiator weighed down by scorn.

Spangled by fresh rain, when innocent air touches.
It lends out a gentle breathe of love, with it the pain smothers.

The ethereal moonlight rents weeping over it,
The flower in despair and dejection chooses not to look above it.

The down cast flower bends long and slender
Though ever-bleeding, has a heart warm and tender.

Girl Child.

They say girls should only play with dolls
But I couldn't hear them over the
Sounds of my imagination.

I can hear a lot more than a little lamb
Or a bit of butter.
I dare to catch fireflies and carry stars in my pocket.

I believe in fairy tales, but also in a bigger
Tale for myself.

I stand tall, not afraid to fall,
Not happy with possessing cherry candy lipstick and Barbie dolls.

I lay not in satins and lace
I shun to be only a picture of grace.

I have hands of steel, not of heart
I can rock the world, sans impudent and pert.

I am a flower not to be waylaid.
I am a pearl - white, pristine and pure.

I am knowledge, wisdom of words, but I am not a book
That is returned and overlooked.

See me standing toe to toe
As I spread my loving wings,
I am a stunner, by Jove!
I am here to stay and not to be disposed.

Mother - My Life.

Hundreds of dew drops to greet the dawn,
Hundreds of bees in the purple clover,
Hundreds of butterflies on the green lawn,
But mother the best gift in my life above and over.

Because I feel that in the heaven above
The angels and elves cooing one to another
None can be found as special as that of 'Mother'.
The divine expression of love.

My trusty advisor, my go-to-person,
A problem solver, a friend -in-need.
You always support and keep me grounded.
Lest when I fall you show me the path to tread.

You are the foundation an inspiration,
I owe my existence to you Ma.

An Ode to the Leiden Centrum Windmill.

Bring the moon over the mill.
As the sun settles
Beneath a blanket made of stars.
Racing the rivers where they run,
The land blooms in various shades of pomp and bright.
I can't but miss watching this lovely sight,
It lies before me like a land of dreams.
So abundant, so beautiful, so true.

Spring of a Different Kind.

The rage of colours,
A spring not so warm,
Fragrance not tantalising,
Frolicking in the heady breeze.

The pandemic raging through,
A fear engulfs minds.
Hopes and desires shaking though.
Love sneaks in crevices, arousing to be kind.

The pain is deep,
The heart swollen and ripped.
Someone with flint and stone crushed life
Lost in the fray, in hospital to be rushed.

Hope now to see light
For we are not going to give up the fight.
All will surely pass
Into the raging passion.
Of a scorching summer,
Of intimacy and satiation.

The Divine Grace—Sarasvati.

I, who am revered since centuries,
Has been a picture of grace.
I, who rests in the lap of Mother Earth,
Flew once and danced in joyous
Swirls and fountains.
I, who am the sister of Ganga and Yamuna,
Got lost in our track to the fertile land.
I, who remain guarded, shrouded in some myth untold.
The confluence at the Holy Triveni Prayag,
Where pilgrims come for ablution.
I, who the ancient referred as Ghaggar-Hakra,
Has housed the world's extensive and earliest human civilization.
I, the maiden sat by the river side,
Lovingly called the '*Veenabaradmanditabhuja*'
With the four strings of the instrument
Striking a chord of harmonics

I, the poet's and painter's muse,
Enlivened in canvases and pages where waves of creativity and mind found avenue.

I, the sacred Goddess of the word spells magic for divine love
I, the manifestation of ambrosia filled goodness
I, the patron of arts and an inspiration to artisans
I, the symbol of pure consciousness with the duck as mound
I, the harbinger of wisdom and cognizance
Counts as a blessing to human mind
Making a palisade of truth, beauty and Godliness.

The Story of a Mariner

Stood on the deck of a ship, a mariner
Handsome and bold.
Never frail and in decision wrong
Upon the waves stand tall his abode
He may be the orb of the hurricane.

The Snow White waves lapped in the craving mind,
Touching beneath the ever- chary spirit.

The beautiful Jasmine laid in an intricate vase,
Enticing her body with aroma of love promise.
The Cinderella of dreams danced in rhythm,
Held him in her soft arms till dusk.
But none could satiate the soul or sweep him off his senses.
The mariner looked beyond
Hoping he would see a world
Where he would find solace even in the house of rocks,
Where soul can reach even when feeling out of sight,
A refuge with its own virtues and merit,
Where the azure of the heavens
Meet the undulating blue below.
The mariner with hope held high
Stood with pride and windows of his heart open wide.
His eyes met a blue dreamy pair
Of the mermaid beneath the sea.
She seemed to wield magic
For she touched the heart of steel
In the heart of the blackest abyss,
Down in fathoms deep crypt,
Where light fails to penetrate.
Her enchanting beauty brightens the world above.
Her intense passion embraces the mariner whole.
He reaches the womb of the sea to meet his heart
Where they have built a nest of love.
Treasure chest of feelings unknown
Engulfed the pair with a visceral longing
Abandoning the hope which he thought forlorn.

9 789354 276088

Printed by Libri Plureos GmbH in Hamburg,
Germany